VIOLENT WORDS FOR BEAUTIFUL PEOPLE

Lucky Ryder

Also by Lucky:

These Things I Crave
Water Media
O.G. Indigo
Inside Dark Light

Contact: sakulryder@gmail.com

Violent Words for Beautiful People

ISBN 978-1-7774688-2-8

VIOLENT WORDS FOR BEAUTIFUL PEOPLE

CONTENTS

CLUBBED TO DEATH

So tonight, I found myself alone, by choice. I lapped the humbling belly bottom of a full cup up to the rim with 90 proof lack of a voice. Parted my lips as my breath set in. I pressed play just to see where the track would go from there. As I downed the last third of the fourth noun turned verb in a similar curve, corked the cab sauv. It was with two spliffs and the first three quarters of the last half of that I heard sounds familiar in the melancholy breeze. Maybe it was just the stoned half cut of my state, but those dead leaf tones rang off the hook with frequencies bent not coincidentally to the naked hips of the triptych of my archangels three. Appendages composed of light alone. Not a second thought brought to my head space for they erased the neck to teach me, and I am learning, truly.

The belts, books, and buckles pages burnt our burden in approximate circumference lasting far from the waist. Scars across your nose your own transpose, bruises on my cheeks. Darker shades fade and wane with the vibration of a classical guitar's fullness until emptiness of the strings. Contused as crystal glass or a woman's voice sonaring between the walls of the chambers of my heart. Their apartment hands twisting hidden blunts in the staired shadows across the street. Only the ember glows enough to reflect off my iris. Palms fish eye in the pupil and rotoscope muscles cope diagonally.

Remember the salves we spread? They're still there and defined in kind we blend in so easily with the cracks in the stained glass. The clouds cover every slab of concrete. Brushes and cans, graffiti tags en francais, je ne sais pas and I must repeat. Carpe diem and a shrouded set of feet. Paintings of mercenaries. No newspapers circulated because we all know what that means. Celestial pelvis in anatomy. A child where my jaw and teeth should be. A ghostly mother fucker, that's what I'll name him. Oblique and bleaker still my cotton mouth grows the crops we need in actuality. Cost and pence and repositioned stance. Slime and a half, an easy dance, a quarter, nickel, dime. Eliminating the buy or the sell. The end or the mid line, or the cut of the hard line. Against the rain, my heart, pours too.

It starts rolling back counter clock wise, numbers diminishing but do not demise. Still grimacing in the old lines, I retrospectively find luxury in the clairvoyance abounding virtuous, but never the purest points of physicality. Pointing towards sacred symptoms; our rituals, we hold in revelry.

My dearest, we didn't discriminate we let it flow just to watch who threw the throwing nest the furthest.

A phoenix born in mid-air.

A man with a woman

in a cave with no home.

An old wolf.

The two grasp the backs of each other's heads. Grapple tightly knotted fistfuls of certainty to tomorrow watch the evolution. The natural will and growth of those twist, sun kissed mitts of thick, and dreaded hair.

DISMEMBERED

She strode back lit beneath the tundra lunar mountains. A rain of combustibles scattered upon the snow and the soft rocks covered. Gambit between her teeth, she ground the suits colors fervently into sparks coffer valuable as the armor we shed together. First the gauntlets, then the breast plate. The gilded slot spattered head piece wheezed distressingly from her chin across brow and off her face entirely. Her spiraling onyx locks hissed, then faded like dying cobras as they came to rest, bouncing counter conquer upon a quivering flag's motionlessness, sped still with a chasing pace.

Limitless spit string stung tranquil guise in stature. Much akin to floating bed posts. The handcuffs glimmered release outwardly to ease in the afterglow of the canopy. Warm and almost skin toned. Remembering the blizzard torched upon them. When our war was haughty and fragrant enough, we were split wide in the likeness of heart monitors off beat, and the Sahara plains horizon somewhere along our tongue's travels from freckled nose to the base of a thick goatee, deep with your scent.

Few happenings on the face of the planet surpass the power to stop time as laughter during sex. Our sounds span me like bespoke baths sewn to fit so eloquently. Their comfort, undeniable. There is certainly no restraint of these things that I do crave.

So I sang songs into her body. Hymns flow up stream filling every space of her being amplified by her extremities and taut cheeks bludgeoned the space coating moans. Bereavement of organic tremulants shattered beyond decibel conception. One would swear this cathedral and bell tower were of ancient stories. Oral traditions kept in the farthest places of her mind. Even the local's memories became fanciful expletives sputtered at a rate fluxed as the stones in the market's open walls. Chisellings of her crucible lower abdominal calls resounding continuously with every drop. Crashing loudly from the court yards.

Fire fountains
and wind falls.

If the cobbled cat eyed scrawls could talk, the priests

swept aside would transcribe tales of public hangings. There hasn't been one in decades but Lordy knows what positions righteous men would bend to bring that blindfold back. So I maintain focus by keeping my ear to the leper's lips for it is at the base of the smoke stack that the coals smolder brightest, and no they don't spit fire or spectacle or call out to speak with anyone in particular; even me, but as they enunciate four looping syllables; 'Alms for the poor.' Resignation as ambient as the black sun's reflection of the clock tower's face onto the empty spaces where the gallows lived. Where the mortar sieved fluent. Their origins being the rock and flagstaff you know trickled here from abroad.

Her broad shoulders lowered comfortably onto solace with the same ease their prophets retold her past as if into the future with such clarity, those stories became synonymous with omniscience. Her ferocity with congruence. My superfluous intention. War calls and bed moans. The space between our heavy mauls proved the mauls themselves, a shield worth erecting.

GASOLINE FOOTPRINTS

At first mind's eye polaroid you fragged me near trench sill dominating traffic. Left airless and a shudder. A childish man, humble asunder on shaky knees.

This ocean of vehicles, so vast, until you caught my gaze and true focus of my winds was not necessary. You were sure to remind me of this as you stood tip toe on the tops of my kicks. As you pressed your breath against the breadth of my lips.

My Chuck Taylors melted down to the sole and blew away like ash.

Reign to overturn, inspire stars derail enrapture comfort and confront me, in the wake of those bar's last opus. Strange since first four stanzas sounded clairvoyant in amongst the dark wood and brass. Droplets sent crimson chaos theorizing between the soft curls of hair and continuing the virtue.

Anti-gravity hand held as analog poetry parted between the blades and dew brings coalescence reminiscent of new fronts approached strongly. The words ran like wine pooling imperfectly. A cup astounds your navel jewellery and running.

Running.

The many body parts your boney hips could be construed as.

Canals.

Channels siphon the sweet between your whispers. Holy ground, silk folds and fragrant incenses. I dare not even speak for the faintest trace slips soft as the farthest stars I know you keep deep, deep, deep, somewhere between stomach and the tail bone's up turned cheek.

When I touch you, I smell you. When I hear you, I taste you. When any single sense is engaged all of my senses experience a love that leaves me knowing what it is to be a part of the self-similarity, I see all around me. To look into your eyes and know that we are the same thing, the same being. To know you know this also, I do not simply lose myself in your eyes. I lose everything in everything else.

There is no vessel. There are no plains, no pains, no vestiges to find round here. No trestles. No dope. No messages. No hope. No kinsmanship, no fear. No threads. No kicks or caps, no happenings, not ever an it is, not a single perhaps. No constraints, no brains, no blue skies, no conflicts, and no remains. To the best of me your tinted windows are a reminder that perfectly personifies what it is to find balance. I lose everything in everything else, and in doing so, I gain what I can only iterate as infinity. The 40 in my bag that never empties. My body breaks down the alcohol immaculately in a last-ditch attempt to penetrate the muscles thread by aching thread. A loss of definition and all reasonable doubt removed within the space of parted lips, and utterance met.

These parameters call vicinity no more accurately than a monk and his cloak equal obsidian deep connection. Now ask me again and I will tell you what is intimate, what is sacred. Ask me again, and I will tell you what is zen.

CRUSHED

As every page folds and tears. As steam rises from paper coffee cups. Mugs overturn. Stains. Set in.

The rain continues and the corners of brick buildings swivel in time and step with your streaming through the streets.

With every parting of my lips, I turn my head to call out to you. A second too late nights still frame shot melancholic slate grey sliver of my crescent moon hope for you.

Just one more time. Just for four more minutes you said. But I'm going to be late if I don't leave. Please stay, we can make love all day long.

I grasp your hip. Bury my face into the crook of your neck. Breathe you in and spoon you as deep as I can just for four more minutes.

Just.

Four.

More.

Minutes.

INFERNO AND THE MIST

There is something about the way I love you from a distance. The viscous resistance. Train tracks attack louder with ever step you take away from me. Thickest from a mountain peak across the valley. Hazy pastel shades degrade massive cliff sides into whatever your subconscious provides.

On this soft morning, bird calls below you, the sound of clouds scraping against and through one another above. That provision comes solemn as apes faces in the mist. Drawn downwards towards the bottomed-out trees like poachers exploding motion. The slashing of forests blemished the beauty marks of these empty spaces and replaced them with cages. Old age passed by in solitude, and lonely. A vantage point graceless even in the presence likened intelligence fortuitous. So tell me what is relative.

The shrewdness of those apes rejected the answers slingshot around the planet. The thick creases in their palms told them better choir songs were the ones written by deaf Africans in the afterglow of the house fire.

Bare foot and tired.

A single dreadlock,
perhaps one of them
named it Panic.

If only the elders had any parables formed from derivatives of what we high rise grown see when the signal falls dead. When the equator experiences frost bite and snow storms, we experience the static. It is only in the dust and shoe print puddles of the metro where I find my partnership with you pragmatic. Without the webs of spinal steel jungle and concrete encapsulate, light dodged as to remind and not forget.

Our solitude is done for.

Clearly, as the enigma's
wet hard hand has practiced.

COPPER

I am conscious of the empty space forever above me. Still, I find myself in the body chamber and am glad that in these days, that means something different.

That the single bulb whose filament had once resounded simply echoed from the rooms of the basement. Bounced from door to bar stool to gathered laundry in the corner, to concrete wall to stair well to window pane and not at all back again. Echoed from the flash of switches blown the breaker. Out into the black night, across the blue and cut a crescent in the atmosphere, leaked out the light.

Girl,
we called that
shit the moon,

until the day it
found the ground.

And I find that the serpents I let coil around me do a lot more than just change color with the bending of my mood from moment to moment. They slither through my nerves and tell me things from the inside. That most of the time seem too intense to begin to try and describe.

I am learning the differences between what I believe. What is living in the shadows, and the beauty of the unknown.

GALLOWS OMEN

I used to be the circle. The vinyl turning perfectly. I swear I would play that track like a murder premeditated, even when on other thoughts it never really goes away. I listen until the finish then rewind to where it began. Only to linger on, spinning on point on yet another moment like linear time has been stolen. I mean on and on and on again endlessly. It would carry on in my head even as I left my bed with the first words and light of day I said. It was there in the background, even as I thumbed my way through the papers searching for my rollies, you know I burn 'em daily.

I took my place on the morning bus alongside early rising yoga students and those still lucid from the night before, the tweakers and the bookies. Their tucked away numbers spelt out the lyrics like closed captioning along the bottom of my sunglasses. There are some secrets that red ink and leather can never hide.

I keep the candles in my eyes few and dim, my vessel free of sin. I glow spectacularly softly. Breath as maiden as the voyage I guess I should have learned to swim something besides the doggy. My backstroke shotty. My singing voice rapid as the breaking notes of knowing there are some songs, that just never crest the waves enough to touch the land before being pulled back out.

The joint roaches sand bag this part of the coast enough to fish tie the cooler waters.

You know it is the spirits of our ancestors that guide land to wet toe side. This is where I am meant to be. The revelry of the tide mixing with the fiery hues pages scorched to ash across the warmer waters. Surely, I have never seen a drop fresh as the whale slaughter since the last night I laid naked on the beach, and cried in time with every tug of the moon's gravity.

My lone light
nodding gently
forever.

A perfect silence.

A flawless blether that lent my pulsing heart's mortality the mechanical simplicity of appreciating whatever sounds bled their way out of the speakers, or out away from the needle scratch.

The subtle noises hold my focus for my ears are as feminine as the lace of audio. Waiting in the wings if only to caress the echo off the curtains sustained by a gender akin to skin spent spoken steady tone enough in length to resurrect passion's own vibrato.

I am here for the quantum physics bred of sound. I am here for the soul's geometry. I used to be the circle until the plain on which the third dimension found me. Now I know I am the spiral. How I know the coil and how rhythm's depth is fractaling.

WAX IN THE WATER

I was the vertices bent by my own conception of surrealism. I blamed the fixation of canvas ablaze on your fascination with Dali. The ladder's corners rounded out to the note of pin pricks tapered a nothing hole in the center. On one end, a vicious syringe. While on the other, the rest of the body protruded endlessly from the molars splayed wisdom ways. Separate the jaw from hate. The deformation from love we called this serpent's mouth.

In lone moments warmed by the crux I had stolen I found entire worlds sung into being by the conviction we held so dear. So near to death we came for the realities of the myths we wrote, but that singeing slit pricks my jugular. Regurgitate my vernacular has rotted one note. Just shut your pretty mouth because this is the first time I have ever had to iterate. Not that if I hadn't, you wouldn't have understood my empty hands. But at this point in time, a banquet of sounds I can only offer. Mirrors that render no reflection. Beauty with no form to sustain it. A song with no ear to behold it.

These are my kaleidoscoping eyes in the rain of color. These are my crying eyes in the black star's sun, shone heaviest on days devoid of ultra violet. I had only the capacity of believing somewhere between sepia and gray scale and a zodiac personified I would ensnare and gift if only you were the kind of girl who would not weep at the constellations caging,

but you are not.

So many things
and nothing I can see.

Light pollution past the atmosphere, some say there was one day not a single one of us did not forget. Wishes what I want for in partners bred our documents manifests. Check marks leave a residue of positivity. What we scrapped from the bottoms bowl trail out far into the Merkabah hour. Glass refines the sands shimmy out in crisp tones we find a secession no longer wanting. For it is the leaving. It is in the flooded sloping under currents where the quantity pulls a second glance. Gloam for glamour stance grades our actions with many, airy, makeshift symbols.

Just so many goddamn numbers, and I cannot continue them all. So I finish strong with whispers we spoke in unison.

"Fuck it all, for we recall the minuscule shapes, the dust rearranged our slop and the acrylics glaze our lips under testament, unlike any rescue we've collapsed."

The bass lines clean themselves now that the art clings to the clouds like it never has before. We let it sleep standing up and leave the wakeful the cushion of the floor.

There is purpose here, so hesitate not a second longer and dose the drug. Bottoms up. Break the banks and when we're caught, I will stick you chest wise akimbo. Er go a lot like the opposite of wounds closing up, and think nothing of it. For I know in the same and single instant you will have roughed a gaping hole in the southern pole of my gut. Fuck.

My shaking tresses still not bodacious enough.

I will take my dying breath four hundred thousand times and square my ruptured lung ad naseum as that it collapses and rises again. Motionless as a turtle's carapace that once upon a time met a carpenter and slowly became a residence. Bay windows that are just the bone and ship wreck frame. Nothing in between. Still condensation accumulates across the glossy eyes. Hand prints that will reappear tomorrow will drift us closer together then I ever thought was safe. My grace will conceal the retracting stilts I wore to walk an even plane from the surface of the deepest reaches of the ocean to the edge of the shore. Your aquatic acquisition and rough carpentry teach me to carve in honesty and my response, will always give me away. In just the right light I believe everything you do. Just the same way that you did. Faith like negative space. The vase and the face. Principles taken as rat poison and lace and other over the counter narcotics all the children take.

Two by fours jammed together with substantial pressure create entire relics without lifting a chisel or nail. No metal involved.

Only, the wood.

Age rings ripple with the swaying of the structure. We move in time with the construction.

Meditating on the pendulum cursive action of ourselves and its relevance to that contrary to our childhood belief, we find development of the land to be a sincerely beautiful progress. Manifesting our potential in a tangible form.

Our intention certain:
I WAS HERE.

Architects heard the rolling echo of thunder storms. They dreamt of coffins and woke to a new understanding of the documentation of sound. Sine waves read in hooked shapes, grasping the side of landscapes from wall to door way. Building men dreamt of where the church met the graveyard and woke to cave openings they saw between their fingers. We closed one eye and breathed through that cuticle space. These were the first mausoleums to house our atmospheres. Our conquest of fears. Our whole truths laid to rest against our half lies. An Atlantis pyramid of sarcophagi laid out the back side as mountains of souls make their way home. Maws longing for the surface and sands fine tide. The windfall current skews the lens through which we under stifled laughter peering wince eyed, jeer in hope that our reflection can possibly penetrate all the way to the ocean floor. Taking every layer masked together along with ourselves recognize transparency as a learning tool. We can take this assault from the waves as a beckoning call that we are the same. That we may all ways see the beauty of the universe in the mosaics we inherently create. For in the dankest depths of darkness we cannot see where we end or where we begin, so we are as endless as we allow ourselves to be. Spoken softly in repartee apart from repetition's reputation as a crooning eye. Stoned spent enough for that what's ripped the start I wasn't sure what I could be.

A bird flown flat lined along the water. Trigger sleeves doused thinner with the soaking. Your sweater of feathers clung heavily to your glowing frame enough so that you resembled the convex splash of the ocean's surface. The sharp edge of glass. The last glimpse of opium from the chamber. The first breath slight as cloud birth. The masticated clash of typhoons, driven and pounded into two dimensions when your clothing contains a lake full flushed. Replenished. Thank you for cradling the divots and that which you know is given. Dissipating as your teenage profile. In my time, I know that mine was thinner. Thank you for allowing yourself to be the vanquishing victims bounty worth of your supple station's vulnerability. Procedures of the new times are the old times accounts. Stacked as smoke stack jackets armor of yesteryear. Determent and sedentary are my pursing lips bloom to the tune of bombs shattering our over coats.

Our silence
is such a conductor.

Lightening tuned in to our frequency alone. Across every

night sky rumors beyond space and time are the electric echo that abounds avoiding ego and that same familiar smother.

Nikola is so jealous he suicides and reincarnates, over and over for eternity in the hopes that he will one day be born again as our only son, a distant cousin, or brother.

DROPPED LIKE DRAPES

Thrice velvet ventriloquism taut time signature. Nine four spread to the snapping of the dropped D's relative clash, touching slightly off center. Oak neck is the better, midnight poison from the battery. Universal like the collective's organic vasectomy of me from what I want to be. A balanced point of the pretense and what I actually need. Pushing me away with one hand free. I grip your other wrist, slit my own with the piano wire tight between your teeth. Our wounds skip beats like shoes in the drier and sloppy stitches. Seething, we lashed our bleeding limbs together like Poe lyrics burnt from the earth up. Seedlings planted backwards begin to blister. We built paths with homes at the ends of them like pistol revolutions. The wright key in the rong lock and other petering sounds you only hear when it's dead fucking silent, and already that's proper. That's loud enough. So sing it again to the broken D string.

I know you can hear me.
I know you are listening.

GUTTED

So tonight, I find myself a lone light nodding gently. Beautifully interwoven amongst the candy apple scent of napalm, rising in the face of the etched concrete level cartoon smilings of multicolored smoke bombs, dissipating to the wind of a new day.

I can only hope that tomorrow I will not feel the same. I can only hope that tomorrow, I will still feel.

www.ingramcontent.com/pod-product-compliance
Lightning Source LLC
Chambersburg PA
CBHW062203100526
44589CB00014B/1929
* 9 7 8 1 7 7 7 4 6 8 8 2 8 *